C000178992

IRISH
BLESSINGS
JOURNAL

The blessings contained herein and others
may be found in *Irish Blessings* (0-517-39989-X),
from Gramercy Books, distributed by
Random House Value Publishing, Inc.,
40 Engelhard Avenue,
Avenel, New Jersey 07001.

O, Ireland isn't it grand
you look–
Like a bride in her rich
adornin'
And with all the pent-up
love of my heart
I bid you the top o' the
mornin'.

May you be half an
hour in Heaven
Before the Devil knows
you're dead.

May you have all the
happiness
And luck that life can
hold—
And at the end of all
your rainbows
May you find a pot
of gold.

Grant me a sense of
humor, Lord,
The saving grace to
see a joke,
To win some happiness
from life,
And pass it on to
other folk.

God needed laughter
in the world,
So he made the Irish
race,
For they can meet life
with a smile
And turn a happy face.

May the hinges of our
friendship never grow
rusty.

An Old Irish Toast

To wish you the luck
o' the Irish, begorra!
Not just for today
But for every tomorra!

May the good saints
protect you
And bless you today
And may trouble
ignore you each
step of the way.

May you always be
 wearing a big, happy
 smile
And really enjoying
 each day
And may all of the luck
 of the Emerald Isle
Always be coming
 your way.

Long live the Irish!
Long live their cheer!
Long live our
  friendship
Year after year!

An Old Irish Toast

May your pockets be
heavy—
Your heart be light
And may good luck
pursue you
Each morning and night.

O, Ireland isn't it grand
you look–
Like a bride in her rich
adornin'
And with all the pent-up
love of my heart
I bid you the top o' the
mornin'.

May you be half an
hour in Heaven
Before the Devil knows
you're dead.

May you have all the
happiness
And luck that life can
hold–
And at the end of all
your rainbows
May you find a pot
of gold.

Grant me a sense of
humor, Lord,
The saving grace to
see a joke,
To win some happiness
from life,
And pass it on to
other folk.

God needed laughter
in the world,
So he made the Irish
race,
For they can meet life
with a smile
And turn a happy face.

May the hinges of our friendship never grow rusty.

An Old Irish Toast

To wish you the luck
 o' the Irish, begorra!
Not just for today
 But for every tomorra!

May the good saints
protect you
And bless you today
And may trouble
ignore you each
step of the way.

May you always be
  wearing a big, happy
  smile
And really enjoying
  each day
And may all of the luck
  of the Emerald Isle
Always be coming
  your way.

Long live the Irish!
Long live their cheer!
Long live our
friendship
Year after year!

An Old Irish Toast

May your pockets be
heavy—
Your heart be light
And may good luck
pursue you
Each morning and night.